GOD HAS NOT

FORGOTTEN YOU

GOD HAS NOT FORGOTTEN YOU

BY

REGINALD T. BYRDEN

www.bookstandpublishing.com

Published by
Bookstand Publishing
Morgan Hill, CA 95037
4231_2

ISBN 978-1-63498-042-5

Printed in the United States of America

This book is dedicated
In Loving Memory
and Legacy of My Grandmother....

Mrs. Bertha J Felder

~ACKNOWLEDGEMENTS~

I give thanks to God for His grace and mercy. Thanking Him for allowing me this opportunity to share this project with the people that I love and with each of you that will read this book. I pray that it will be a great blessing to you.

There are times when we go through life and it seems as if we are all by ourselves, even when we are in the company of others. I say would like to you that no matter what it looks like, always remember that God Has Not Forgotten You.

I am grateful for my wife Dorothy who has been a great supporter of me and this Ministry for the past 20 years. I am grateful for my children Tymicia, Tyandra and Regan Alexis, my granddaughter McKenzie and my Godson Eric.

I am grateful to my Mother Ms. Mildred Byrden, for all of the love and support that you have shown me. I could never repay you.

My Grandmother the late Ms. Bertha J. Felder, whose constant faith and caring and loving hands nurtured me early and kept my focus on what really matters.

I would like to acknowledge my loving and caring Aunt Ms. Dorothy Lawrence, who played an important role in my upbringing, and my Aunt Ms. Mary J. Arthur, who has been very supportive to this Ministry.

I am thankful for a loving and supportive congregation, Grace Fellowship Church of Columbia; I thank each and every member for your love, prayers and outstanding support that you have given. I am honored to serve as your Pastor.

To other family members and friends, I thank you all for your love and support. I am grateful for all of my mentors and teachers who have poured so much into my life.

I make no claim of ownership or originality in these pages. What distinguishes them is that I have been able, by the mercy and the grace of the Lord, to prepare them for your ear and edit them for your eyes as you read the words on every page. It is my prayer and hope that you will be encourage and enriched the more as you take the time to read every word and turn every page.

Thank you for your support of R.T.BYRDEN MINISTRIES. Be Blessed!

TABLE OF CONTENTS

~*G*od *H*as *N*ot *F*orgotten *Y*ou~

Tucked away in a quiet corner of scripture is a verse containing much emotion:

> *"FROM THE CITY MEN GROAN AND THE SOULS OF THE WOUNDED CRY OUT."*
> ~Job 24:12

The scene is a busy metropolis filled with speedy, noisy movement. It's covered by rows of buildings, apartments, houses, restaurants, stores, schools, cars, bikes, and children.

1

All that is obvious is easily seen and heard by the city dwellers and all present. But....there is more. Behind and beneath the loud splash of human activity are invisible aches. Job calls them "groans". That's a good word for it. The Hebrew suggests that this groan comes from one who has been wounded. Perhaps that's the reason Job adds the next line in poetic form, "the souls of the wounded cry out". In that line, wounded comes from a term that means "pierced". However, he is not talking about a physical stabbing, for it is "the soul" that is crying out. Job is speaking of those whose hearts have been broken. He's speaking of those who suffer from the blows of "soul-stabbing"; which can be far more bloody and painful than a physical stabbing. Can't you just see it.... The city, full of the sound of the wounded, bruised, and broken, groaning from the heart?

Does this describe you? If not you, perhaps someone that you know. There are people living with the memories of past sins or failures. Though they may have confessed and forsaken those ugly, bitter days, the wound still stays red and tender. They wonder if it will ever heal. Although it may be unknown to others, they live in the fear of being found out.... Of being rejected.

Whether openly or in secret, we all are, have or will endure wounds. We will all experience scars. This is a good thing!! God in all His infinite wisdom allows us to go through scaring situations in order to elevate us. You see, scaring is proof that healing is possible. God is our HEALER!! ONLY He can heal the pain and sin of our past and make us whole again..... And He WILL!! You want to know why? I'm glad you asked!! It's because God LOVES YOU SO!!! And NO MATTER WHAT, you have to know that *God Has Not Forgotten You!!*

Reginald T. Byrden

~*L*ose *T*o *W*in~

S he couldn't even look in his face as she repeated vows after the Pastor. It just wasn't right! It didn't feel right, didn't look right.... It wasn't right. She knew that this was not the man that God had called her too. There was this thing in her. Stubborn....probably. Naïve....some. Hardheaded.... DEFINITELY!! Her Mother had spoken with her slightly. Not in a pushy way, but just to get her to think. "Marriage is a serious thing, and not to be taken lightly sweetie. Being equally yoked is of GREAT importance! But more than anything, you need to seek God's face on this one. If you don't, and you marry someone that God did not ordain for you, you will be filled with sorrow. God's way is always best! Don't ever doubt it!"

Oh, how I wished I had listened and not blown my Mother's words off. She was oh so right! The sad part is.... I didn't even notice. Well, I did, but not in time to avoid the hurt, the pain, the scars that I will carry for the rest of my life.... Oh no.... not even close. It wasn't until he started hitting me to the point of bruising, broken bones, and bleeding that I noticed that he had an anger issue that was multiplied by alcohol. It wasn't until my daughter started asking "where does daddy live" that I noticed that he wasn't a family man. It wasn't until my friends started fading away and I had more time on my hands than I knew what to do with before I realized that he had driven everyone close to me away. I REALLY just didn't notice....

I prayed and prayed profusely for God to deliver my husband, for God to fix my marriage and heal our wounds. It seemed the more I prayed, the worst things got. One Sunday, I asked my husband to come to church with me. He declined as he usually did. I went on by myself feeling lower than a bowlegged caterpillar. *"God, I'm calling on you because I feel low, I feel lost....God I need you right now!!* You see what he's doing to me, to our children, to our family.... Can you just get'em? Guess what happened...... Nothing!! I called out to and begged God for years after that time. One day.... I heard the voice of the Lord clearly. "You did not seek my face concerning this man....You did not seek my face concerning this union. Why daughter, do you choose to get yourself into these situations when you know that my plan for your life is perfect, all you have to do is trust me. This is not the husband that I designed for you. This is the reason that you are out of commission." I heard these words clearly, but I was too stuck in the "but", "what if's" and the "I want". I was so afraid of starting over, of failure, and of "loosing" that I stayed in this situation for many years. In that time, I even tried to fight the voice of God with my own "understanding", only to continue in a loveless marriage with no hope......

I began to fall into despair! I just didn't want to lose what I had. What I had was empty and lonely... but it was what I had. I wasn't used to anything else. I was afraid that I would never make it on my own; that I would be a failure once again. I told God all of my fears one day as I was walking in the mall. I must've looked like a lunatic to everyone around me, but I didn't care. I needed to get it out. I couldn't take it another minute. As I walked into a boutique, I heard a song that was a little familiar. For some reason the music brightened my spirit. It seemed that I listened to the entire song, but I only heard seven words. The words were "Sometimes you gotta loose, to win again". I felt peace in my spirit. I knew that this was not the love that God wanted me to experience. I knew that this wasn't the man that God had designed just for me. I knew that I did not ask God anything concerning this man and that made me question what I already knew was showing; and that was that I did not REALLY trust Him.

You see, sometimes, it is necessary for God to allow us to experience let downs and disappointments so that we will know that He is God. Sometimes we have to learn that our plan

8

is not better than God's plan. He will lovingly allow us to go through the stages that we need to go through in order for us to see who He really is. God does not punish us. I mean, think about it. If God was REALLY trying to get you back for all that you've done or haven't done..... Do you really believe you'd be able to stand it? God really has not forgotten you!! You are the apple of His eye! He loves YOU as if you were His ONLY child!! Can't you just feel the LOVE! He wants NOTHING less than the best that life has to offer! However, He's not forceful or pushy. He's not going to try to make you fold and bend to fit his plan. He's going to give you the opportunity or the choice to trust him completely. So why not do it today?

~God Has Not Forgotten You~

Afterthoughts:
Forgiving = Forgiven

When people you love let you down, it can be so hurtful that you can wear the bruises for years. For this reason it is so important that we lean on God's word for understanding. We are by nature a very selfish people. More times than not when we hurt someone or have damaged a relationship, we do so without considering how it will affect the other. It is not until the damage is done that we review our actions. If you are honest about it, you will agree that you have hurt someone else; sometimes intentionally, other times you may not be aware. Still, you have caused some hurt. If it was in you to apologize or try to make the situation right, your ultimate goal was to receive forgiveness, right? If you don't receive forgiveness, you feel bad just knowing that your actions hurt someone in the way that it did. With that in mind, do you believe that your forgiveness is more important than that of the next persons? Do you think that you've been so awesome that you should be forgiven but what the other person did was so hurtful that they do not deserve the same?

Well, guess what...

~You have to be forgiving in order to be forgiven. Sure others will do things that may hurt you to your core.... But take a look at the life of Christ.....~

Jesus was talked about, lied on, beaten, spat on, humiliated, persecuted, nailed to the cross, and left there to bleed and die for YOUR sins; but in the end He still begged his Father in heaven to forgive the people that had come against him. If our goal is live Christ like, it is so important that we develop a heart that is able to forgive. You can walk around holding grudges and disliking people all your life if that's what you want, but you are only hurting yourself by making that decision. When you forgive....I mean TRULY forgive, you are releasing the hold that the enemy has on you. Who wants to be bound by the enemy? I know I don't!!

Pray with me

~Father we come to you humbly thanking you for helping us in the area of forgiveness. We thank you now for the perfect example that you sent to us. We ask that you help us to develop a heart that is able to forgive and we thank you in advance for revealing to us the error of our ways~

Amen.

~*F*laws and *A*ll~

~The Bible NEVER flatters heroes. It tells the RAW truth about each one. If a man is a liar, it says so. If he is a crook, it says that too. The Bible always tells the truth about men so that we can magnify God in His act of grace on the platform of human weakness~

David was an adulterer

David was a murderer

There he was in ANOTHER mess. He turned and noticed her. She was the only woman…the only human alive that was still in his corner. She was always there no matter what. She always had something encouraging to say. He watched her as she sat there. She was always murmuring something and holding that little cloth. Her "prayer cloth" is what she called it. He could hear her through her tears with all that "rumble-a.. rumble-a- rumble-a. He never understood what she was saying or what she was doing. He didn't even really care. He was just happy that someone was there. The pound of the gavel brought him back to his new reality just in time for him to hear her speak. "Excuse me your honor....You know me well. This is not our first time here, but it will be my last time here with my son. I have been in constant prayer and meditation concerning him. May I please address him before you take him? Please sir, this may be the last time that I get to speak to my son." The judge looked at her and motioned for the attorney's to approach the bench. They whispered briefly and both nodded in agreement. The judge then motioned for the woman. She approached the front of the courtroom. "Son, I have loved you even more than I've know I

14

was capable in this life. I nurtured you, comforted and cared for you as best I knew how. I prayed and prayed for your deliverance and NEVER, EVER gave up on you. I have always been in your corner and I always will be. It wasn't until a few minutes ago, while I was in prayer begging God to spare you once again. I pleaded with God to soften the heart of the judge and the people that you have harmed. In the midst of my praying, I heard the voice of the Lord saying; "Not this time. He will never come to me if you are always in the way. He will go through things in order that he might see my face and I am separating him from you so that you will see my face. If he does not choose me, I cannot heal his land. Son, I love you with my whole heart, but I have to give you to God and let Him work on you." The son's face was turned up. He didn't understand what his mother was saying to him. Truth is, he didn't want to understand. It sounded to him like; she was turning her back on him. "Ma, what are you saying to me right now?" He asked her as the tears welled up in his eyes. She shushed him. "Son, I've been diagnosed with congestive heart failure and stage 4 pancreatic cancer. I've been sick for years son. You didn't even notice because you've been in your own world, doing your own thing. And that's ok. I should not have been trying to fight God's battle in the first place. I probably won't be around when you get away from this one, so I want you to hear me son. Work on your relationship with Christ. God LOVES you so. He created you to be a KING. He didn't make you to be no thug. Give yourself to God. He promised me that you would lead many to Christ. Regardless what it looks like son, I'm standing on the promises of God and believing in the only name that matters!! The only name that delivers, the only name that sets free, the only name that redeems, the only name that can correct you and keep you....and that is the name of Jesus! I have to leave you son, but remember whose you are. God is faithful. Get in position and stay in position. I love you son...I love you!!" The guards pulled the son back from his mother. They were not allowed to touch or embrace each other.

The son was escorted to a holding cell until he was transported to the prison that he would spend the next fifteen years. The mother turned and walked away. She faded away until there was nothing there but the memory of her..........

The son had wallowed in self-pity for years at the death of his mother, neglecting her words. Those words he heard from her took him through every emotion imaginable. He was tormented for years about the things that he had selfishly put his mother through. In his mind, the stress that he had put her through had driven her to her grave. He really didn't even notice that his mother was sick. He began to look at himself....REALLY look at himself. He saw the filthy wretch that he had become. He saw how he choosing to sell drugs had poisoned mothers, fathers and families in his community. He saw how his absence and selfishness had caused his children to suffer to no end without the influence of a father in the home. He saw how robbing people had stripped them of more than material possessions. He saw how the lies that he told hurt those that REALLY loved him. He was a mess. He was a felon. He was a deadbeat Dad. He was a prisoner. He was a lost cause and not the "King" that his mother thought. It must've been her illness that had her delusional. There was no way that he was a representative of ANYTHING royal..............

The son began reading books. He noticed a copy of the bible. They had even given him a copy that he so thoughtlessly tossed aside. There was something that was drawing him to this book. Something he couldn't really understand. After a while, he stopped questioning his thoughts. He just picked it up and cracked it open. He started reading the book of Psalms. There were new things dropping in his spirit. Things he knew nothing about. Things he didn't understand. This "God" and "Jesus" that his mother had always been talking about was starting to look real to him. He couldn't believe it. Maybe..... Just maybe his mother was on to something.

He read Psalms repeatedly. He was floored. God knew about ALL of David's flaws, but He STILL chose him as the

"King". He was beginning to understand what his mother was trying to say to him. It couldn't be possible that God meant this about him too. Yes.... He had done all those things that David had done, PLUS some. He had messed up more times than he could count, but....... Could God REALLY use someone like him? Could he REALLY be chosen to do something special for GOD? His thoughts turned back to his record.... His record had shown almost all of the terrible things he had done. People looked at him like a thug, a deadbeat, a criminal.... What could he possibly do that would please GOD with all that he had going on? He continued to read. The more he read, the more the words of his mother came back to his remembrance. The more he read, the more revelation he received. Every single time that he read, he had a brand new thought or idea that God was really who He said he was. More importantly, HE was who GOD said he was. He changed his mind about him on that day. Because of that, this was also the day that changed his life............

Afterthoughts:
Covered By The Blood

Our minds at times will take us to a place that is in such awe of the work of the Lord in our life that we began to see the situation with eyes that are not like God's eyes. I'm sure that you have visited and revisited that pity party concerning that thing that you did to hurt someone, that lie you told, that $20 that you shorted God on your tithe, that wife/husband you cheated on, that thing you said in anger, that money you gambled away, or whatever it was. Even if you committed a heinous crime; grace and mercy is extended to us all! If we are living under the "law" which is the Old Testament then sacrifice is what is required for sin. But as a believer, we are privileged to live under the BLOOD OF JESUS. Jesus was sent to teach us, to lead us back to Christ and to cover us from the filth of ourselves. Because of this "covering", when God looks at us, all He can see is the blood of Jesus or our sacrifice. God *doesn't see your sin, because it's covered under the blood. So we can celebrate today because no matter what our situation or our battle God is not concerned with that. God is concerned with your heart! If He calls you home today, what will he find there?*

Pray with me

~Father in the name of Jesus, I thank you now for the covering of me under the blood. You know my faults even greater than I know myself, yet still I hear you calling my name. Still, you love me. I'll never understand why, but I'm glad you do! I receive my "ouch" today and I am ready to let go and surrender all this mess that I've created trying to do this thing on my own to you. Thank you for giving me another chance to follow your will for my life and for your patience. Your grace is truly sufficient! I love you with my whole heart!~

Amen.

~*God's Love* OR *Man's Love*~

I grew up in the typical household in the ghetto. Single Mother, five children, Absentee Dad, Section 8 housing, food stamp fed, welfare recipients….. Like a lot of those families, we had a very key thing missing. The struggle created such sadness. We had no joy. My mother did everything in her power to shield us from the negativity of the streets and raise us right, but there was something missing from the equation….. Our Dad….. Our Dad was BIG in the streets. Everybody knew him and loved him. Everybody except us, that is. All we knew was what we heard from other people. When we would tell our Mother what the people would say, she just nodded and changed the subject. Often times that motion would come just in time for her to catch the tears that would've been sure to fall had she not. Other times that pain turned quickly to anger and disgust; still she NEVER talked down on him or allowed us to talk down on him. She was always saying that our Dad would come around and things would be better. I never really believed her and I'm glad that I didn't because I would still be waiting on him to "come around". I refused to spend my life waiting and longing like she did. I LOVE my Mom and I still hate to this day that she died loving a man that never loved her back. It was always crazy to me that she never gave up on him. She never, ever tried to replace him. She always stayed to herself and if she was ever seeing another man, we never knew anything about him. It's really, really sad now that I think about it. Here was my Mother, a beautiful woman, smart as she can be, talented, loyal, strong and loving; sitting there her entire life putting all her trust in this one man that came around as it was convenient for him to do so, giving her a false hope.

He ran the streets as he pleased, played around with multiple women, showed up when he pleased, played over my Mother's emotions and her mind until her heart just couldn't take it anymore. Watching this as a young man and not being able to do anything about it was horrible!! How could my own Father... My REAL DAD, destroy the woman that nurtured his own children in this way. She trusted him completely with the best part of her. The part that she could never get back. She opened up her heart and her soul to him. He did not realize or appreciate this gift. He had no appreciation for her sacrifice. He left her there feeling used and alone with a house full of children to take care of. She didn't have the opportunity to go off, try to get her life right and her finances in line before she was able to figure it out. When we needed anything we looked to her PERIOD. He left her PERIOD and didn't look back. I guess some good did come out of it though. I was able to learn from my Dad what a man was NOT supposed to be. He taught me well about what I would NEVER ever be to my children, my wife, or my community. If I could ever thank him for one thing, I'd thank him for that! He was a beast at teaching it and operating in what I guess he would call "tough love". All these emotions took over me when my Mother died. The Doctor's couldn't find anything wrong with her, but everybody knew that she had a broken heart. It's strange to me how we will allow others to steal our joy. Joy can only come from God. Unless you make a "being" your god, how can they take that which they did not give in the first place? You would have to give that permission by making them your god. Is that the kind you want to serve? God is the only being that can restore that joy. Whether stolen or given away, you have to know that if you plan to get it back, you will have to submit to your first love. You may believe that God just left you out there with your broken heart, your situation or your circumstance, but what actually happened was you turned that person, those material possessions, that job, etc. into your god. God loves you so!! HE would never forget about you. Just think about the

26

Bible. God is not a man that He should lie, right? His word is true. He would never leave you out there to fend for yourself. However, God is NOT pushy. He's not going to make you come to Him for ANYHTING! He's not going to make you believe His word, or force you to trust Him. He will lovingly allow you to find your way. It is God's hope that you will come back to your first love. That you will receive the gift of life, of peace, of joy, of understanding and of LOVE!! This LOVE cannot be duplicated or replaced by any human. Believing so will leave you living a life of disappointment and despair. God will NEVER leave you nor forsake you!! Don't be like my Mother, living a life of sadness looking to someone who is incapable of this kind of love. Instead come back to your first love and NEVER forget He who has NEVER forgotten you!! Nobody can love you like God!!

Afterthoughts:

We can go a whole lifetime looking and looking for love. We put expectations on what love is to us based on what we've seen in the home or on TV. But what we see with our physical eyes is no true representation of what love is. Think about the love that God has shown us. The first thing that comes to mind is "sacrifice". What are you willing to sacrifice for love? Do you make sacrifices for love or is it just a lip service. Would you kill your only child? Of course not...... How about different sacrifices? Would you kill a habit, lifestyle, thoughts as a sacrifice for love? Love is not what you see up on the big screen....it's what goes on behind the scene that REALLY shows your love. Do you know the LOVE that God is showing for you behind the scenes? Well, let's take a look it..... You woke up, you walked, you talked, you can smell, touch, eat..... Do you know that God worked those things out for YOUR TODAY before you were even a twinkle in your Dad's eye?

Now THAT'S LOVE!! You can search the whole world over twice and you'll never find a love like God's.

Pray with me

~Dear God, I thank you so much for loving me! It is because of your love that I even know what it really is. Had it not been for your love, I would never have really experience love in its purest form. You are so amazing. I pray that I can display love to your people in the way you've nurtured me with it. I thank you for making me your priority and keeping me there like I'm your only child. I love you back!~

Amen.

~*T*he *T*wo *R*eports~

My son is kind of a shy kid, at least when he first meets you. He has to get a feel for people. He sits back and observes his surroundings, paying very close attention to detail. When I say he notices EVERYTHING, I mean everything. Once he gets a feel for people and his surroundings, he very slowly and very carefully monitors their behaviors. He once told me about how he categorizes his friends. He said that this helps him to get along with everybody, not just certain ones. Sometimes people can get in cliques and just limit themselves completely from anything new. My son found away in his nine year old mind to love all people no matter what the difference. We could all learn a thing or two from him. I laugh, at times, at the level of maturity that he possesses. God knows he didn't get that from me!

This year we moved to a different area. This transition is especially significant because, I'm a single Dad of two, raising a son and a daughter on my own. Some might think that this is no big deal.... But for me, it's everything. I've never experienced a thing like this before in my life. You would think that I would struggle with my daughter more. Honestly, nurturing her is a LOT easier. I grew up in a home with a single mother myself. Although, I had male influences in my life, being surrounded by my sisters and my mom made it easier for me to understand women, their emotions, and they're mannerisms. One big thing that I picked up was learning the body language so that I would know how to move when they didn't say anything. I must say that this was a great thing for me to pick up; otherwise, I'd be doomed!! My son on the other hand was quite the opposite, not because he's a bad kid. It's just that in some very big ways, he's very different from me.

I was a happy –go-lucky kinda kid. I did my own thing and didn't care much what people thought of me; for the most part. I didn't really fit in with others outside of my family, so I was comfortable in my own zone. As long as I had my cousins, my brother, my football, and my games; I was totally satisfied and content on my own. It wasn't until I was a teenager that I realized that I was what some would call, weird…. More like, a nerd. Erkel was my nickname for years!! It wasn't until about 9th grade that I shed that title and became "Stephan". My transformation came overnight. I didn't even notice how fast it happened or even when it started. One day I was the cute little geek whose brother was a great athlete. The next day I was on the girls most wanted list, a beast on the football field, and I could sing too. Those things brought on a whole different set of "friends" that I had not previously been privy too. All the flirting, compliments, and accolades quickly went to my head. I won't say that I became conceited or developed a proud attitude, but I was definitely feeling myself. I liked the new me.

There were a few things that slipped through the cracks that made me look suspect. Like the music that I liked. I wasn't really into rap like the other boys, but I listened to it as to not stand out. I didn't really do the baggy jean thing, but every now and then, I managed to pull it off. I wasn't a promiscuous kind of guy, but if I didn't follow up the ladies advances; that was another blow to my new status and a threat to my new "A List" friendships. So, there I was in my "UNcomfort" zone, playing all these rolls for all these people. It wasn't long before I didn't know myself. I had camouflaged God's creation so many times, with so much STUFF that wasn't me that I had lost sight of who He had created me to be. You would NEVER believe the struggles of finding yourself with hurdles like that to jump. It was almost like I had developed multiple personalities trying to please everybody else. I had been so busy trying to be who "people" said I should be that I had no appreciation for the gift of "me" that God had given those same people. I REALLY didn't see that God was grooming me to minister in any way. I never thought that He COULD use ME for anything. There was the report of man that said that I was a chump, that I was ugly, that I was nerdy, that dressed like a geek, that the things that I LOVED were for lames, that no one would ever love me, that I was a wretch undone, that men didn't deal with children like I did, like my voice didn't matter, and that I needed to tuck myself away in the deepest corner and hide the embarrassment of a man that was me from the world. Yet, here I am today, with my same bubbly personality, silly mannerisms, million dollar smile and khaki slacks working with children in the church, counseling and nurturing troubled teens, and ministering in song. WHO KNEW?? God knew; that's WHO! Which report will you believe about you? Word to the wise: God is ALWAYS right…………

Reginald T. Byrden

Afterthoughts:

Why is that in life we jump so many hoops to please others, live like others, BE like others? Trying to be like someone else is like telling God that He made a mistake when He made YOU. Yes, you can shake your head RIGHT HERE, because GOD does NOT make mistakes. How could you believe such? You are wonderfully AND fearfully made! Don't ever let the report of the world tell you any different. God's design of you was one of purpose. He made your eyes, YOUR nose, YOUR legs, YOUR EVERYTHING , the way that He did ON PURPOSE with a purpose. You have to know that you ARE God's gift to the world. He loves everything about you. He gave you the gifts that you have on purpose. He wanted you to walk the way that you do. Although the world may view you as invisible, God views you as impossible to miss. To Him, you shine bright like a diamond! Won't you believe God concerning you today?

36

Pray with me

~Oh God, How GREAT thou art. You have so lovingly taken your time with me. You've molded me into what stands before you now. I'm sorry that I did not acknowledge your infinite artistry. I am ever so grateful for your artwork that is me. I am grateful that you took the time to mold and make me in your likeness. Never again will I belittle or allow anyone else to belittle the king in me. I am perfect the way that I am because you made me and I thank you for it!!~

Amen.

~God Has Not Forgotten You~

Reginald T. Byrden

~*What Is It You Think You See?*~

It had been eight years since I step foot in a church. For some reason on this day, I just wanted to go more than anything; so I did. Travis had been inviting me to visit with him for months. I guess it was guilt and shame that kept me out of the House. It had been so long since I had been back. The club and night scene had become my favorite past times. Endulging in my habits was my way of life and without that, life was... well....boring. I had become the life of the party. I was accepted and not judged. Everybody knew what to expect from me because I had been so faithful in delivering. I heard my Grandmother say, "You always come back to what you know". I guess this was the reason for all that tough love from my family. But then, a new thing happened. I had lost my connection with the local hustlers, so my finances fell off. I went from being the life of the party and the one that everybody came to when trouble stirred, to being the one that needed those same people in my hour of desperation. Oh, the truth in my situation hurt me. I mean, it really hurt me to my core to see the realness of those whom I had considered friends. It never dawned on me that maybe I was being used or maybe I was the one that needed the help. It sure was crystal clear at this point. Now that it was clear and I realized how foolish I had been, I feel into a sort of depression. I had put so much faith in people, in money, in material things that I had lost sight of my own prize. I wanted to ask God to help me, but how could I? After all of the things that I had done to defile the sacrifice of Jesus, all the cursing, partying, drinking and drugging, lying, stealing...... How could I possibly set foot in the House of God? I would probably explode in a ball of gaseous flames as soon as I walk through the doors. My thoughts kept me away for so long.... Still I longed to be in the house. On that day, I stopped worrying about what people would say. I needed to be in the House.

It took a lot for me to get dressed and get to the House that morning. I made every excuse in the world not to. First it was, I don't want to go by myself. I called Travis and told him I wouldn't make and that was why. He laughed and said I'll swing by and pick you up in a hour and you can go with me. Well, that didn't work. Then it was, "I don't have anything to wear! People will be staring at me!!" Travis must've know this would be next, because he walked in with the cutest little black dress that he bought for me. Then it was, "We're gonna be late! I don't want to walk up in there at Noon!" Travis very calmly explained that the service didn't start until 12:30! I just gave up! Nothing I tried worked! So maybe that was where I was supposed to be.

This was probably the longest most uncomfortable ride that I had ever taken in my life. I thought I would just die! I trembled as he opened the door for me. I didn't know what to expect. We were greeted at the door and seated. From that seat I watched the whole fiasco. This guy stood up and Sure enough, as soon as Praise and Worship was over, I was ready to flee! Praise and Worship was more like a group of people in a church doing two selections and a theme.... Ya'll know how that works. There was no praise and no worship involved in what they did. A man that appeared to be holding some special position in the church got up. He started talking with the congregation about the Bishop and all the wonderful things that he had done for the church and its members. He went on to point out specific families in the congregation and let everybody else know how the Bishop had paid their light bill when their lights got cut off that week. He reminded them of the family that had lost their home in a fire and how the Bishop had put the family at his home until they got situated and how he had bought them a new wardrobe. My face was balled up by this point. "I wouldn't want him to help me with NOTHING if he's going to be putting you on blast like that with the whole church!" I was guessing that this was the man's usual announcement before they took up the offering. Do you know that the offering took almost an hour!! I wasn't a Bible scholar or anything, but I know that God gives everybody free will. So in other words, once you know what you're supposed to do, the choice is yours. The Bible talks about your tithes and offerings, but an hour coaxing people to give their ALL to the church was ridiculous! The man started with $100. He said that he felt in his spirit that there were fifty people that wanted to give $100. The word "Tithe" never came out of his mouth. He had the men and the women line up on different aisles. I was floored! I was REALLY regretting coming to this place. They went on down the line with $75 from twenty five people, then $50 from fifteen people, then $25 from ten people. When they got past the $10 people, he said "Now everybody else." That was my queue I was with the "everybody else" crew. All I had was ten dollars, but I was going to give God his ten percent plus my offering. Just when I thought that it was over, that man came back again saying that he felt that there were some people out there robbing God. He cautioned them on their behavior. You would not believe it, but at least fifteen more people got back in those lines crying as they held their monies in the air. This was my first time back to church in over EIGHT YEARS!! Even though I was undoubtedly the BIGGEST sinner in this place, even I knew that this was wrong. I would never be up in a church with that mess. It made me angry to see how they were doing God. The church was a respected zone for me even though I didn't frequent too often in those days. That experience had me wanting to step further and further back to what I had really come to believe. And that was, why in the world should I be coming to church when this is the kind of hell that goes on there.......

When the Bishop walked out on the pulpit, some people actually did pass all the way out! They bucked, hooped and yelped for almost thirty minutes at his presence. I could not believe my eyes! Do they think that he's God himself? I was saddened seeing how the members of that church would get up and run full laps around the church and pass all the way out, laying across the pulpit or even right on the floor at the mention of the name of the Bishop. I couldn't believe how all of these seemingly educated people could believe that this Bishop had some kind of power that could measure up to the power of God. Just then one of the ushers or guards at the door, if you let me tell it, grabbed me by the hand. I pulled away from her, but she already had reinforcements. A second guard appeared out of NOWHERE! The two ushers led/forced me up to the pulpit. So I just gave in. I didn't want to embarrass Travis. This was our first time coming to church together. Travis looked up at me from the organ. We both looked terrified. The Bishop began putting some kind of oil on the people's heads that were at the altar in the shape of a cross. When he got down to me, I stepped back and said "No thank you." He paused and looked me over. He looked back at Travis as if to make some kind of gesture. Travis stopped playing and immediately walked over to the Bishop. Out of nowhere, the Bishop lunged at him. He knocked Travis to the floor. Travis got up, went back to the organ, and started playing as if that didn't just happen. My mouth dropped to the floor. I looked at Travis with a puzzled look, but he would not look at me. No way in the world, is what I was thinking! If he thought for one second that I was about to accept the same punishment, that robe was going to be flying all over this church." Oh, I got to get up outta here!" Other members surrounded the people at the altar. One by one the Bishop said some words in their ears, the next thing you know they were hitting the floor. BAM! When the Bishop got to me, he mumbled something in a language that I didn't understand and then said "Blow on her Lord, Blow your winds on her right now in the name of Jesus." He stepped closer and started that chanting thing again. I guess he didn't get what he was looking for, because he moved on to the next lady in the line. Before I could blink, that lady was dropping to the floor like a limp noodle. I moved out of the way and the lady's head hit the side of the pew. The usher looked at me with disapproving eyes and said, "Why didn't you catch her?" I looked back, "I didn't know what was going on, I thought she was in the arms of the Lord." I laughed at myself for that one. The usher clearly found no humor in my attitude and stepped back so that I could go back to my seat. I made a B-line to the door and NEVER set foot back in that church again.......

Afterthoughts:

This may sound terrible to you, but I learned a few things. One, was to stop looking at the actions of PEOPLE and start focusing on the WORKS of God. I was so worried about what the people would say about me bringing my little backsliding self to church. This situation helped me to believe what the Word of God says and that is that we ALL sin and fall short of the glory. This also taught me to stop putting so much focus on the "POSITION" of man. Yes, this man was the leader of this flock and yes he was to be respected as such. But all the GLORY belongs to God and God alone. At times, we fail to realize that the leader of the flock is STILL just a man/woman that has accepted the call to serve in ministry. Accepting this call does not mean that they don't have struggles, don't get angry, don't have disappointments, don't feel saddened or troubled, don't get hurt or have problems. In fact, accepting such an assignment would make them more vulnerable to these types of attacks by the enemy. We at times, put the "title" before our "relationship" with God. When this happens and the man/woman of God falls to their human side, we get so touchy. This is not the time to throw stones. This is the time to lift up the man/woman of God in prayer. No man is perfect, the Bible tells us this. Still we expect the man/woman of God to be blameless. It is true that we trust our leader to lead us in the right direction, but truth be told, when it is all said and done; God will be looking at YOU and your actions. Who/what have you made your God? Is it that Pastor that you're praising, that man or woman that you're chasing, that "money over everything" mentality, that job, that car, that credit card, that home, another persons' life? Be mindful of the titles and what you are praising. All the praise and glory belongs to God alone. God has not forgotten you.....Be sure that you don't forget Him!!

Pray with me

~Dear God, You have provided for me exceedingly and abundantly above what I could ever ask or think. You have done this over and over again despite my ungratefulness or my unworthiness. I thank you God for not seeing my flaws as man does and for molding this broken vessel into something beautiful. Please help me to be appreciative of what you have blessed me with and to wait patiently on the time that you bless me with more.~

Amen.

~*B*linded to *S*ee~

He was only five years old when they found out that he had Cancer. He had been a sickly baby, from chest rattling coughs to vomiting and the shivers. His mother had taken him to every specialist in the state that she could find. None of their "possible diagnosis" made any sense. None of the medications gave him any relief. None of the treatments panned out. Still, nobody could find out what was wrong with Shaun until then. Money was tight and that hindered a lot of the progress. Mother prayed and prayed that God would heal her baby boy. She went to church after church. She poured out her frustrations to multiple Pastors. Entire church families fell on their face asking God for healing. She surrounded her son with prayer warriors. They stood strong by her side believing that whatever God was up to would be a great testimony; the greatest testimony that the people of this little town had ever seen. Sharon had VOWED that God would be at the forefront of her everything after all of this. Mother had not been what most would call a saint, but she had nowhere else to turn. God was not her first option, but she quickly learned that He was the only one that could heal her son. Even as hopeful and prayerful as she had been, healing was not what happened for her son. Baby boy got even more sick as time went on. She didn't understand what was going on or why it was that her baby had to suffer the way that he did. She went to church like they had told her, she studied God's word, burned up her knees praying, put all her fleshly desires to the side, stopped partying, drugging and drinking....still nothing changed for her baby. Where was this GOD that everybody was going on and on about? He sure wasn't showing up for her baby. She began to get angry.........

Sharon's anger took her in the direction that everybody was sure she would take. She didn't care, nobody knew what she went through trying to buy medicines and pay for doctor visits that price tag exceeded her measly little Pizza Hut salary. Nobody knew the night that she sat up trying to comfort her son when she had to cut his dosages in half so that they would not run out before the end of the month. Nobody knew how hard it was to have to ask her neighbor to run the extension cord from their house so that she could cook for her son when the lights got cut off. There was a lot that Sharon had to juggle to make sure that Shaun was ok. So there she was a broken woman, working her fingers to the core to make ends meet, caring for her son without the help of a husband or father. She did what she knew would help her. There was no leaning on God. She had been there and done that. The only thing that had gotten her was sore knees and nosey people in her face. What they offered didn't help her son and didn't help her. In her mind, this was the equivalent of someone telling you that they're hungry and you telling the person to pray with you. She had a hunger that was not being met and that was all that she saw. None of those "church folk" knew what she was going through. It wasn't long before she pushed that to the side too. Going to church and wasting endless hours talking to God wasn't putting any more food on the table. She had to make something happen.....

Jeron had made her an offer that had been a challenge to refuse so many times that she felt confused as to why she was REALLY trying to hold out. Shaun needed medicine, she needed money...seemed like a no-brainer. There was something holding her back from it all. She fought the good fight as the Church Mothers had told her and that got her ABSOLUTELY NOTHING. Shaun was still sick, she still didn't have the medications that she needed, she was starving, her bills were going unattended to..... She'd had it with all the Holy Roller crap. She needed a baller..... A few of them. She called Jeron up.... That exchange was easier than she thought.

Apparently, there was a high demand for woman that didn't have anything to loose and didn't care about losing…..

There she was… out with the next random guy. She had broken her body so many times that she no longer recognized herself. The "church folk" stayed in her face throwing scriptures left and right. She didn't want to listen, but somehow she heard them. By this time she had birthed baby number four with ANOTHER random. She fell deeper and deeper into despair. The only peace that she had was the fact that Shaun got what he needed. Even though she now had four mouths to feed PLUS her own…. She was making the money to do it, so she swallowed her emotions and did what she thought she had to do……

"I made a promise to you that I have already kept, all you have to do is rest in that"…..Those words woke her up EVERY night….taunted her every thought… interrupted her days…..She just couldn't get past those words. Those pesky little Church Mothers always had "A Word from the Lord", but never had any clothes, shoes, groceries, medicine, or MONEY! She never understood how they could be so content with not having what they needed. She would never allow herself to struggle again or her children to suffer regardless of what she had to do to make it happen. She just refused! She continued to travel her way........

She couldn't believe that she was pregnant AGAIN!! Baby number FIVE and once again, she had NO CLUE who the Father could be. Of course a big belly is not something that can be camouflaged forever especially when it's been swollen as many times as hers. Sharon fell to her knees. She just looked at all these little people that were depending on her to get it right. Here she was doing it all wrong. She cried out, God I need your help!! I know that I'm your least favorite girl, but I don't know what else to do. I don't know where else to turn. Look at all this mess. Why did you let me do this to myself!! WHY!!! Where are you!!!

Baby number five came and Sharon's body became less than favorable to the "ballers" that she had put so much of her trust in. Not only was she torn down in body, but also in mind and spirit. As she looked at her life she saw the mess that she had created. She thought that she was fixing it by going out there on her own. What she got was a band-aide on a bullet wound AND more trouble than she could handle. When Shaun died, that just tipped her over the edge. She screamed at God for stripping her of her son. She had loved him more than her own life. She had sacrificed everything for him. She had scarred herself forever and GOD just snatched him from her!! She couldn't believe it was happening to her.

When all of the children went to sleep, Sharon grabbed her coat and walked out of her house. The air that brushed against her cheeks felt warm which was weird for January. Let her tell it, it felt like somebody had kissed her ever so gently on her cheek. It was an innocent gesture. She felt warm and loved. Even with all the pain she had endured. She closed her eyes and took in the moment. God knows she didn't get many like that. She opened her eyes just in time to notice a lady walking in her direction. She peered through the shadow of the street light to see if she could recognize her. But she had never seen her before. She wasn't afraid, but it was strange to see a stranger on that street. As she met the lady she noticed a sort of glow around her. The woman looked so beautiful to her. As they passed the lady stopped and spoke to her. "God just wants you to GET IT". If you can ever wrap your mind around this, your life will be more amazing than you could ever imagine. Your house, your finances, and your children are blessed! Be well, beloved." Sharon just stood there wondering what to say or think as the woman turned and walked back in the direction that she had come from. Sharon looked around and the woman was gone. There was that kiss again. There was a peace surrounding her. She was convinced that God had heard her cry and sent an angel to help her understand His plan........

Afterthoughts:

Often times we get so focused on the outcome of a thing that we forget that it is God who is really in control. For this reason, it is so important for us to keep our eyes on God and not allow things or circumstances to block our view. That thing that we are facing, that tragedy we're walking in, that prayer that we've been praying.....God knows about it, He hears you, and He has already handled that in his own way. It is up to us to trust that He will do JUST what He said. No matter what it looks like, God's plan is still better than yours. If we would all just stay out of God's business of our lives, we would begin to see our breakthrough that is JUST around the corner. We could literally take the next step and fall into our breakthrough, but we fail to REST in the promises of God. Lean not to your own understanding, but in all your ways, acknowledge Him and He will direct your path.....

We MUST stop putting our trust in man. The only one that matters is God. God is THE ONLY one that saves, delivers, sets free, purges, blesses..... Why then, are we leaning on those that could not REALLY help us anyway? God is a Jealous God..... He even says it in His Word; that we are not to put other gods before Him. That doesn't necessarily mean a pagan god. It could mean anything that you lean on and put your trust in, there by worshiping that thing/person. By doing so, you have given away so frivolously the one thing that belongs to God. Don't you want to give credit, where credit is due?

Pray with me

~God we love you. We are so sorry that you've had

to watch as we choose people and things before you.

We will take this lesson and hide it in our hearts. We

will not allow our focus to be wavered. You have

shown us more times than we can count that your

love for us is solid as a rock. Please, help us to

receive your love and trust you completely!~

Amen.

Reginald T. Byrden

~Needs vs. Wants~

As a college student it was odd for me to receive mail since I went home every weekend. Can you imagine my shock and excitement when I discovered an envelope in my box? I grabbed it up and ripped it open. It was like sparkles flying in the air. I couldn't believe it. It was too good to be true!! It had to be too good to be true! There was no way in the world that someone would send a broke College Student a Credit Card with a spending limit of SEVEN HUNDRED AND FIFTY BIG ONES!! Especially not this one!! They had me messed up!! I made my way up to the dorm and sat on the bed surrounding myself with all of the paperwork that came along with this card with MY NAME on it. I didn't know anything about percentage rates or anything.

All I saw was that these people, whom I knew nothing about, sent me a card with money on it for me to blow. The letter said to call a number to activate and to start spending NOW! I knew what my Mother would say about it, so I decided to keep that little detail to myself. Besides, I was a college student now. I really SHOULD have a credit card. I needed to establish some credit any way. I was an adult now. No, I didn't have a job, a place to live, insurance, or even a vehicle; but a credit card was a great move, I just knew it!! This seemed legit to me, so I called the number. The lady gave me all the information I needed and after a few moments, she let me know that my card was activated and I could begin using it immediately. I must've sat there staring at that card for the better part of an hour. I was still mesmerized and in deep thought about ALL of the things I was going to buy…….

I packed my things and headed to VA for the weekend. I gassed up my car and got on the road as soon as my class was over that Friday. It only took me four hours to get there. I crashed a friend's couch and we partied like rock stars the entire weekend. I had a new outfit every time we went somewhere new. I was showing off by paying for everything we did. There was some kind of POWER that I felt every time that I swiped that card. My friends were amazed that I could do what I was doing. The showered me with more kudos and pats on the back that I had EVER received in my life. I guess that seven hundred fifty bucks wasn't as much as I thought it was. By the time I got back to school, there was only $62.44 available to me. I had no clue where all that money had gone. It must be a mistake. I called up the card company; I was ready for a fight. Well..... That's not what happened. I set them straight alright...... I got my little booty handed to me. Sure enough, it was me that had gone on a swiping frenzy.

A few weeks later, I got my first bill. YIKES! I had no clue what I was going to do with that mess. So I just tossed it aside. Did I think about it again?? Not even!! I withdrew the last few dollars in the balance through the cash advance and tossed that card in the DEEPEST corner of my junk drawer. You will not BELIEVE what happened next!! I went to the mail to see if they had sent me another bill since I had not paid it on time. Sure enough they did, but THREE more companies had sent me Credit CARDS!! You would THINK that I would RUN with all my might to the garbage and dispose of those little plastic demons. Instead, I RAN ever so frantically to my dorm, ripped open the envelopes and activated them ALL!!!! I had already been consumed with the POWER to swipe! I had no limits. I was a 19 year old college student with no bills, kids, or responsibilities. I had time and NOW I had money. I took full advantage of both. In a matter of about two months, I had maxed out SIX credit cards. I justified my spending habits by saying I needed this or that. When the bills came, my willingness and ability to pay was pretty much non-existent; yet I owed. What had seemed like a God-send in the beginning turned about to be a nightmare that would take me YEARS to wake up from!

It's so easy to get caught up, when it looks like you can get something for nothing...... Believe me when I say, there is NO SUCH THING! Jesus told His disciples that they had to work for what they got and to not take more than they needed. They were not to "catch a sale", but let their "yes be yes" and their "no be no". It is NEVER wise to try to live beyond your means to the point that you become a slave to your transactions. We should all work with what it is that God has given us and WAIT on the time that He elevates is to more.

Reginald T. Byrden

Afterthoughts:

Oh, if we can ever learn to be grateful!! Life would be as smooth as a babies back side!! God loves to reward us with favor in whatever area He deems fit, but if we don't allow Him to direct our paths, how can He REALLY lead us to our overflow?? Sometimes you can block your own blessings by putting yourself in the way. Material possessions get old, out dated, worn, and then they have to be replaced. Why would you put so much on "things" that will never sustain you anyway? Take responsibility for YOUR mess. If you owe somebody.... Pay them!! If you say you're going to do something....DO IT!! Just like people, God is going to take you at your WORD! God is not going to leave you by yourself, but know; Faith without works is DEAD!!

Pray with me

~God I thank you for all that you have done, what you're doing, and what you will do. I recognize my own greed and I receive my "ouch" today. Please God give me the wisdom to recognize the difference between a need and a want and not sacrifice my integrity in order to obtain material possessions.~

Amen!

Reginald T. Byrden

~Managing Life's Detours~

I'd like to talk to the sinners. Yes....that means YOU!! We all fall short of the Glory therefore we are ALL sinners. There is hope for us as believers, but there are still some that do not know the TRUE power of God. It is our job (the believers) to be examples to them in hopes of bringing one soul unto the truth.

By being examples of God's love....... Even in un-Godly places in our lives whether that is in a physical or a mental place. We have been challenged by God to be a representative of Him wherever we are. That is from the pulpit to the streets. No matter where we are in our walk, there is always an opportunity to be a witness. Being a witness just might save some one's life, but more importantly, it might save some ones soul.

It is my desire at least to have my actions help someone make the decision in their hearts to turn to God.

The scripture talks about laying aside every weight or sin....

This is so relevant because sin can hold us back from doing those things that we were called to do. There are also other things that may not necessarily be sin- but weight, that are mere hindrances that can keep us from successfully or effectively running the race that God has for us.

Our choices are not always between what's right or what's wrong but also between what may or may not stop us. In other words premarital sex or more appropriately, premarital sin is a sin that could delay you from your works. Just as the weight of worry or fear could keep you from your works.

Apply this to your own lives..... Is there a weight that you must lay aside to get to where it is that God would have you to go?

Is there a sin? One that so easily besets you?

Besets..... That word can be broken down four ways.

1. Easily avoided

2. Admired

3. Ensnaring

4. Dangerous

The sins that are easily avoided are just that..... Very easy to avoid. There is that free will thing. God gives us the authority to make that decision. We can simply just walk away.

There was a young lady that had a problem with stealing. She was in a store with her sister. She was unemployed at the time and school was about to start. Her son needed some socks and t-shirts. They were right there for the taking and she knew that she could get those things and more out of the store without ever being detected. She could get away scot free and nobody, not even her sister would be the wiser. She remembered the only Bible verse that she knew. She said to herself, "The Lord is my shepherd, I shall not want." Even though that was all she knew, that was all she needed to know. She walked around that store reminding herself that her Father had all the riches that she needed and all she had to do was ask. When she got home her sister handed her two bags. When she looked in the bag she saw three packs each of t-shirts and socks for her son. The other bag had a few packs of paper, some folders, pencils, crayons and a ruler that was inside of a back pack. She had "easily avoided" that sin that had so easily in the past beset her. Because she trusted God in her moment of weakness, He had provided for her abundantly above what she had hoped for.

We may not see it but these are the times that God is looking to show us that He is GOD. If we allow Him, He constantly and very lovingly shows us that He is with us through it all.

Some sins are admired, but must be laid aside if we are to walk gracefully into our destiny. Everything that glitters ain't gold. We have to take our sights off of the things that are of this world and remember that there is no greater reward than getting a home in glory.

There was a young boy that grew up in a family that was dirt poor. It was five children with just their mother to support them as their dad had left them to make it on their own. Their mother being very sickly herself did the very best she could do for her children with what little she had. The young boy grew up promising himself that he would never ever struggle the way that his mother had. He started at a very young age working whatever small jobs he could find. His meager salary could not help his family's situation. The fast life was looking sweeter to him by the second. He met some of the wrong people at the right time and before long he was a King pin in the drug game. He had saved and saved several hundreds of thousands of dollars and was on his way to becoming a millionaire. One night as he slept peacefully on the luxurious bed that his money had afforded him, he was awakened to a raid on his home. He had found himself alone and running out of the money he had fell so deeply in love with. The love of money had landed him in this place. He spent ten years in a federal prison thinking about what all that money had really bought him. All he really needed was God and with that came True love, perfect peace, and anything that he could ever need or desire.

Though material things are admired, they can never sustain us. The only thing we can count on in this life is GOD. If He has to sit us down to see that, He will.

Some sins are especially harmful, these are the ones that we should run to God with and take cover. Yet, these are at times the ones that we run to.

She always noticed the woman coming into the store. She noticed her because she would always come three to four times a week. The woman was always beautifully dressed and would always spend several hundred dollars on her purchases. She always wondered how she could, in this economy, afford to be spending like she was. The more the girl watched the more envious she became. She had almost become a stalker. She even got angry when she noticed how sad the woman looked. One day she asked the lady what she did for a living. She told her that she was a stripper. The girl was totally amazed. Here she was breaking her back for twelve dollars an hour, and this woman had it all! She wanted it too. She went down to the club in her most provocative gear in hopes of snagging her a job. She got so much more than she had hoped for. There was a guy that had presented himself as the owner. He had invited her to do a private audition for him and two of his colleagues. That night she was raped by the three men. She was left beaten and bloody to die. Two months later she woke from her coma to find that she was pregnant and also to find that she was HIV positive. You never would know by looking at that woman that she had suffered the same fate and was now fighting with all her might against full blown AIDS that she had contracted herself. We must learn to be satisfied with what we have. You may admire the things that others possess, but you never know what it cost them. God blesses us all in His own way and in His own time. Don't get caught up in all the STUFF....God is King, that makes YOU royalty. He will deal with you as such and reward your faithfulness.

The dangers of sin go without saying. When we dress ourselves each day, we have to also remember to put on God so that we might have the insight to see these things and the power that he gives us to avoid the outcomes.

We must endure!

In Acts 20:24, Paul pictures himself as a runner who had a race to finish. Nothing would keep him from finishing this race with JOY.

God expects the same from us. That we not only finish the race but with JOY. That can only happen through endurance.

Jesus is the best example. We must keep our eyes, hearts and thoughts on Christ. He is, or should be our focus, our inspiration, and most importantly our example. We have to be careful though as just seeing him as an example, because He is so much more. He is the ULTIMATE example of endurance.

Phil 1:6 says, *He who has begun a good work in you will complete it until the day of Jesus Christ.*

How encouraging is that in times of discouragement??

This is the JOY that we can look forward to. No, Jesus did not see the cross itself as a joy, in fact he despised it. But He could see past the horror of the cross to rejoice in His crown that was beyond that.

What keeps us from bearing our own cross? Well, at times the biggest element of torture in our own cross is the shame in it. For most, this is a huge stumbling block. We will do just about anything for Christ except endure SHAME. We get so caught up in what our families might say or the opinions of the church, our community, our peers, or colleagues that we forget that the only opinion that really matters is that of GOD.

Even though we know in our hearts that it is more shameful to be bold about our own selfish needs in this life, we still cower when it comes to boldness in the will of GOD.

Why is that??

Compared to Jesus, we have not endured anything. He died on the cross for the sake of us all. He was pierced in His hands, feet and His side. He was hung and left to bleed and die and all this for no fault of His own. There have been some that would not give up some of their lunch so that someone else could eat. Never mind dying for something that somebody else did.

We are not asked to give our lives, but to share our lives and our testimonies for the good of others so that God can get the glory, but we are afraid and for what? I felt that way at one time, but now I realize that it's not important what people think or say, because I know for myself where God has brought me from and I want to share it with the world.

If it had not been for God, Where would YOU be right now?

Consider Jesus..... Had it not been for this sacrifice covering YOU for your mess, what would God really be seeing when He looks at you?

Because He could endure through the cruelest of punishment, the bloodshed, the torment, the shame, being criticized, beaten, maimed and mocked..... I can surely endure these little trials that life presents me with. So, no matter what it is today or any day....Don't ever forget about God, Don't ever forget the LOVE, Don't ever forget the SACRIFICE!! He did it ALL JUST FOR YOU!!!. Know that God has not forgotten you and He NEVER will!!

CPSIA information can be obtained at www.ICGtesting.com
Printed in the USA
LVOW04s2328090415

433874LV00003B/4/P